She be

She be

TINA PISCO

bradshaw books
Cork, Ireland

Bradshaw Books
Tigh Filí
Civic Trust House
50 Pope's Quay
Cork, Ireland

+ 353 (0)21 4215175
info@tighfili.com
www.tighfili.com

ISBN: 978-1-905374-18-2

Cover design by Tina Pisco ©Tina Pisco 2010.
Typeset by John Noonan

Printed in Great Britain by MPG Books Group, Bodmin & King's Lynn

Acknowledgements

My thanks to Mairie Bradshaw, who has been on this poetry journey with me since giving me my first reading in Tigh Fili, McCurtain Street fifteen years ago to publishing this collection. She has been a true friend, guide and mentor. My thanks also to Fidelma Maye and Aoileann Lyons for their cheerful support and for Aoileann's eagle eye.

Thanks to Sue Booth-Forbes, along with Tigh Fili, for giving me a week at the idyllic Anam Cara Writers and Artists Retreat in September 2009. I could not have dreamed for a better start for this collection.

My thanks and gratitude to poets Ian Wilde and Kathy d'Arcy for their careful reading and edit. You made me see the work in different lights and helped me to finally tame the words until they agreed to sit on the page.

Finally, my thanks to all the people who inspired these poems: from the anonymous black guy in NYC to my beloved, John Noonan.

To Juana, mi Abuelita
Esperanza y Pilar, her daughters
Alexandra and Patricia, their daughters
Chloé, Amelia, Sasha, Francesca, Cristina and Paola, our daughters
and all the women yet to come.

Contents

WOMAN

Photograph   2

A Housewife's Lament   3

Magic Dance Fountain   4

Bum Deal   5

DOGFOODCATFOOD   6

Contradictory Expectations   7

Aller Simple   8

Flaunt it!   9

From St Andrews to the St Alixe   10

Lillith   11

Ça ne Rime à Rien, ton Histoire...   12

Exhilaration   13

She be   14

The Quincaillerie de mi Alma   15

Vero's Bolo   16

She Took Care of Them   17

A Modern Mitochondrial Myth   18

Go Home   21

THINKER

Start of Summer   24

Valentine Poem   24

5ft 2 and a Size 24   25

Contrails   25

Not so Crazy on 8th Avenue   26

Sky News Over Bantry Bay   26

Hips in St Andrews   27

Cork Apocalypse   27

Perfect   28

Contents

LOVER

Leaving Blackrock   30

I've Already Loved you Forever   31

Rêves de Venise   32

Catnip   33

La Niña Milagrosa   34

John's Panama hat   35

Lonely Heaven   36

Conundrum   37

Safe Haven   38

WRITER

The Strap Hangs Ready by the Door   40

Advice to a Creative Writing Student   41

You Won't Find this One in the Bible   42

Anam Cara   43

Ten Steps to Stay Sane   44

Cork's Changed   46

Saltimbanques   47

Artists' Exemption   48

Wallflower   50

Not a Cigarette   51

For Sharon   52

WOMAN

Photograph

The American students pose
in front of the National Museum –
three rows of shiny hair and perfect teeth.

She kneels in the middle of the bottom tier,
smiles at the camera, fresh faced, well groomed.
"Say cheese!" says their teacher, taking the shot.

And suddenly I see
another girl, not born yet,
not even conceived.

She picks up the silver-framed photograph
from the mantelpiece,
points to her mother and says:

"That was in Dublin on her senior school tour.
Can you believe she was ever that *young?*"

A Housewife's Lament

What honour is there
in retirement from
a life making things tidy?

Where is my golden clothes pin?
My mounted broom?
My trophy dish cloth?

Will my husband and kids
even notice that I'm gone
before the laundry piles up
and blocks the front door?

Where is my Adonis,
tickling my veil
with feathered fans,

dangling grapes above my lips
as I lie back, contented
and content, on a bed of roses?

I take your white
Y-fronts from the dryer
and fold them once again.

Oh, I could tell you more
of my pain, but
it's time to collect the smallies

from playschool.

Magic Dance Fountain
for Chloé

You are a magic dance fountain
Where acrobats gather to celebrate.
They somersault, leap and roll,
do handstands below as you pirouette on a spume of inspiration.

Punters gawp at the spectacle
high above them; trapped by your eyes
flashing green through silver droplets
as you twirl. And they wonder: "How do you do it?"

They who can only shuffle, crawl and creep.
They marvel as you leap
over heartache and joy.
Once for the girls. Twice for the boys.
Dancing to music they cannot hear.

Bum Deal

I want a wife who'll think of me during the day.
Who'll ponder what I'd like to eat when I am far away.

And are my shirts clean and is my suit collected?
I want a wife who'll search 'til every speck of dirt's detected.

I want a wife who'll sweep and dust and polish stairs.
Who'll juggle kids and work and me like coloured balls up in the air.

Who'll stock bananas, juice packs, school lunch snacks.
I want a wife who'll give up her life and never look back.

I want a wife. One who really cares.
Who'll feed my kids and make my bed.

I need a wife. I got a husband instead.

DOGFOODCATFOOD

Dog food. Cat food.
Bread. Butter. Milk.
Soap.

Dog food. Cat food.
Bread. Butter. Milk.
Tampax?

Dog food. Cat food.
Bread. Butter. Milk.
Burger Buns.
Fairy liquid.
Instant Coffee.
Fruit and yoghurt.
A new mop.
Veg for dinner.
Snacks → school lunches.
DROP BACK VIDEO!!!

Some days are special:

Wine (3 red/3 white). Beer.
Turkey. Bread crumbs.
Cranberry and crackers.
Port. 2 lbs of butter.
A litre of cream.

Some days are slim:

Mince. Milk.
Toilet paper.

I write more shopping lists
than poems. I write them every day –
shopping lists, not poems.

I write a poem every now and then,
but I write shopping lists
every day.

Contradictory Expectations

Who said:
Cross your legs
Smile sweetly
Don't shout
Don't run. Walk
Don't talk back
Don't ever be alone in a room with a boy.

Who said:
Stand proud
Be anything you want to be
Don't be tied down
Free your body
Never give up
Keep your feet on the ground but keep reaching for the stars.

Who said:
Cook like a chef
Fuck like a whore
Take it like a man
Look like a babe
Kiss it and make it all better
Guys don't make passes at girls who wear glasses.

Who said:
Fight for what's right –
but don't make waves
Hold your ground –
but don't be too forward
Respect yourself –
but look like her
Love with all your heart –
but not too much.

Aller Simple

for Amelia

I bought a one-way ticket
for the first time in my life.
Aller Simple, no return

and felt deep in my heart
strings snap as I knew they would

the minute they handed you
to me, I knew
some day you'd leave.

And so tried to remember,

to savour, to cherish
to relish the flavour
of each passing hour

of each passing day
of each passing year
that brought us closer to that parting.

I bought a one-way ticket
for the first time in my life.
Aller Simple. A simple go

and sent you on your way –

ma petite fille,
ma petite chérie,
mon Amélie.

Flaunt it!

Don't kill it
Don't squash it
If u b woman
Embrace it!

Don't stifle it
Don't chain it
In the cold, dark dungeon of ur heart
If u b woman
Feel it!

Don't hide it
Don't veil it
Ashamed of the power of ur face
If u b woman
Show it!

Don't cover it
Don't bury it
Under paints & powders & polite conversation
If u b woman
Flaunt it!

From St Andrews to the St Alixe
cento for Sasha

Waiting in the St Alixe,
thinking about St Andrews,
I sit and watch
the *trique billiard*, silent in the corner.

The radio blares French pop
as I toy with a *pinche* of Primus
and eavesdrop on the drunks who sit and chat,
or stand at the bar and argue.

And then I remember I promised you
I'd write a cento about:
The stupidity of wood. The watchfulness
of shoes. The indifference of sons.

A poem made of stolen lines
that resonates with the echo of footsteps
through towns where Weather is a citizen
whose wide birthright is sky.

But I am lazy and bored
and listening to the drunks
who sit and chat,
or stand at the bar and argue

and to the tinkle of the cash machine
and to the French pop blaring
and to the silent *trique billiard* in the corner.

A man has noticed me. He winks:
"*Une bière pour Madame?*"
I smile and accept.
Relieved of my burden,

I wrap up my plundered poem,
store my words in salt,
and promise to attend to it
when I am once again 15 miles from civilisation.

Lillith
for Niamh

Behind the mirror
In secret caves
Deep in the Earth

In Summer's heat
In Autumn's blaze
Through Winter's death
For Spring's return

Behind the veil
For rent or sale
Shackled in silence
To sing again

Down in our cells
Dark in our dreams
Until we wake

She waits

Ça ne Rime à Rien, ton Histoire...

We sit in the dark
by a window and wait.

Though no one is coming
No one is there,

We sit in the dark.
We sit and we stare.

We sit in the silence
Repeating one line,

Longing for meaning.
For rhythm. For rhyme.

How?
How *could* you?
How could *you*? You! . . . Do THAT?
How could you do *that*?
To *me*? Me!

How could you do that to me?
How could you do that to me?
How could you do that to me?

We sit in the dark
by a window and wait.

Though no one is coming
No one is there,

We sit in the dark.
We sit and we stare.

We sit in the silence,
Repeating one line,
Searching the rhythm
For reason and rhyme.

How could you do that to me?

Exhilaration
for Francesca

You know the feeling you get
when you jump into the sea?
When you jump into the sea
you get this *feeling*.
You know that feeling?

Like when you're racing your bike.
You get that *feeling* –
like jumping in the sea.
You know that *feeling*?

When you're racing down a hill. Or skiing.
You get this feeling.
You know that *feeling*?

Jumping into the sea? Or racing your bike.
Or skiing? Or running real fast?
You get this feeling:

Like your heart's gonna burst
and your head's gonna pop
and you don't

ever,

ever,

ever,

want it to stop and then suddenly

it's gone.

She be

She was tired
She is tired
She be tired

and relentless, dayafterday
Everyday
24hrs ain't enuf

To get it all done
To keep it together
To stop it from falling apart

It seeps here,

dribbles,
a little here,

leaks   over there . . .

Some days the floods rise
The dam breaks
A finger won't do
She can't stop it from spilling over

She holds her breath,
suspended in the moment
after the glass leaves her touch and before it shatters on the floor

Some days she sails
She soars
She swoops and plugs the crack in time

A hug, a kiss, a mallow cake
and for a minute forgets
how tired

She be

The Quincaillerie de mi Alma

I love enamelled pots and pans.
Speckled blue bowls and cups.
Kettles whistling on the home range.
Coffee singing: Don't fence me in.

J'aime le fer blanc. Hachoir.
Passoire. Bouilloire. Cafetière.
J'aime les carrés rouges et blancs
dans la cuisine de Bonne Maman.

Me gusta una buena paellera,
y una cuchara de madera
marrón y negra de los sabores
en la cocina de mi Abuela.

Y una caldera, y un sartén.
Casserole et poêlon.
Terrine and cake tin.

Mortar and pestle.
Bread bowl and sauce boat.
Chopper and crusher.

Smelling of garlic.
Seasoned with age and oil
and the memory of marvellous meals.

In the language of my
kitchen, mi cocina, ma cuisine,
where form and function meet,
I see only beauty.

Vero's Bolo

Just in the door, she goes straight for the celery, carrot, onions, garlic.
Chops them fine. She adds a dash of pepper. Throws in a pinch of
memories and only then takes off her coat, talking all the time.
    "He's moved out, you know? He says he needs some space."
She pours in the tomatoes, spices; dips spoon, tastes. She tastes again,
frowns, spoons in sugar, salty tears. "I can't believe I gave that bastard
my best years." The water's boiled. She chucks in pasta, wipes hands,
eyes. Goes to the hall and yells: "Girls! Dinner's ready!" Comes back
and checks her pots again. Sits down. Sighs.

She Took Care of Them

She took care of her mother,
her father and an elderly aunt.
Her young friends and her old neighbours.
Her church and her school.

She took care of the plants
and watered the flowers.
She took care of the dog and the goldfish
and the hamster named Ted and the stray
cats at the bottom of the garden.

She took care of her family:
She took care of their clothes.
She took care of their meals.
She took care of their sheets
and their towels, and their duvet covers.

She took care that their shirts
were pressed and their shoes
were polished and their vitamins
were taken.

She took care that their hair
was clean and their ears
were scrubbed and their teeth
were brushed.

She took care of what books
they read, how much TV
they watched and whether a PG 15
was appropriate.

She took care of: one Barbie shoe,
one piece of Lego,
a single unclaimed key.

She took care of: a rubber band,
a length of string,
a scribbled phone number.

She took care
and put them aside.
"Just in Case."

A Modern Mitochondrial Myth

Though every human receives half of their DNA from their father,
and the other half from their mother, the mitochondrial DNA passes
intact from the mother to her offspring. Thus every mother's daughter
carries the same mitochondrial DNA as her mother's mothers' mothers.

I.

Her name was Moira. She was a warrior.
She had a sword. She could fight.
She could win. One day a great army
was going to rise and fight with her.
She lived hard and she loved hard.
She could drink, fight and love with the best of them.

She got knocked up.
She had a baby girl.
She named her Gayle.

Gayle was a leader. She had been taught
by a warrior. She had a vision.
She could talk to people. She could make them listen.
She had a man. His name was Seamus.
They stayed up all night,
drinking and talking and making love.

Until she got knocked up.
She had a baby girl.
She named her Lola.

Lola didn't want to fight.
Lola didn't want to lead.
Lola didn't see the point of doing anything
much really (except buying lots of clothes,
and going to lots of parties). Lola was a bitofabimbo.
Most of all Lola didn't want to have a baby.

She left her little girl with her mother
and ran away to become a showgirl.
Before she left she named her Monica.

Monica was a dreamer. She was taught by a leader.
Monica could talk to people. She could make them laugh.
Monica had a boyfriend. She made him laugh.
She saw there was something weird about this whole
"Sun spinning around the Earth" thing.
He thought that was hilarious.

She got knocked up.
She had a baby girl.
She named her Amanda.

Amanda liked to listen. Amanda liked to laugh.
She had been taught by a dreamer.
Amanda liked to think. She liked to drink.
She was a drinkerthinker. She got incredibly drunk one night
trying to explain why she liked thinking so much
to this really cute guy called Nils, who seemed really interested.

"I think therefore I...? OH MY GOD!"
thought Amanda just as
the first labour pains hit.

She had daughter.
She named her Marilyn.

Marilyn liked looking at things. She liked measuring things.
She could study things. She could learn.
She'd been taught by a drinkerthinker.

Marilyn was a student. So was Bob.
They started studying together. They shared a room.
They put the bassinet in the corner.

Marilyn named her daughter Judith.

Peeping over the wickerwork,
Judith watched her mother studying.

II.

She –
knocked up –
a baby girl –

Moira, Gayle, Lola, Monica,
Amanda, Marilyn, Judith

a warrior, a leader, a bitofabimbo,
a dreamer, a drinkerthinker, a student,

had a sword, a vision, a man,
a boyfriend, dreams, thoughts, a daughter,

taught by a student, a drinkerthinker,
a dreamer, a leader, a warrior,

to study, to think, to dream,
to laugh, to listen,

to fight, to win, to drink,
to lead, to see,

to talk to people, to make them listen,
make them see,

things, looking at, things,
measuring,

her mother,
watched, her mother,

who could, liked, lived,
loved, was, had

a baby girl
who got knocked up.

Go Home

Go home and tell your husband.
Go home and tell your kids.
Go home and drop your burdens
On the floor, in a pile, with the laundry.

Tell them: Who you are -
Who you were - Who you could be.

Go back and tell your mother.
Go back and tell your Dad.
Speak gently and remind them
Of a time, of a girl, dimplefaced, laughing.

Tell them: Who you were
Who you are - Who you could be.

Go home and drop your burdens.
Go home and greet the sun.
Go home and face the mirror
Of a new day, in a new life, with a new you

And remember: Who you are -
Who you were - Who you could be.

Go home.

THINKER

Start of Summer

Lying in the bath, I look
out the window. See
the first swallow;
and think:
"It's time to shave my armpits."

Valentine Poem

"What have you done for me lately?"
I ask on a grumpy Valentine's eve.
And then remember your kisses on my neck
and the way you take me in your arms
every day. And how you tell me you love me
all night, every night;
and think:
"Blessed. I am blessed."

5ft 2 and a Size 24

Walking fast down Princes' Street, I bump
into a fat chick coming out of Top Shop
who looks depressed;
and think:
"Bet she couldn't find anything that fits."

Contrails

Sitting on a rock, blue sea below me. Blue sky above.
I see a white contrail streaking West to America. Spot
the dot containing 300 souls;
and think:
"I wonder if they're serving dinner?"

Not so Crazy on 8th Avenue

Eating lunch in Mickey D's, I notice
a black man, nodding and talking to himself,
carefully dispose of his tray;
and think:
"That guy's not as crazy as he looks."

Sky News Over Bantry Bay

Sipping a cappuccino, I spy
a mute TV screen filled
with fire and death;
and think:
"I should call home."

Hips in St Andrews

Slim girl with wide hips. I watch
her tracksuit sway;
and think:
"When she has kids she's gonna take up half the pavement."

Cork Apocalypse

Dodging the raindrops on Pana, I steer
clear as a flood of ostriches sweeps
past in the bus lane;
and think:
"It'll be raining frogs before we know it".

Perfect

Waking late on a Saturday morning
I drink coffee at the kitchen table, listen
to the purr of the Aga, watch the trees
shiver in the stillness, feel the heartbeats
as The House sleeps;
and think:
"This moment is perfect."
"This day is perfect."
"This life is perfect."

LOVER

Leaving Blackrock

Warm smells.
Soft skin under my cheek.
Scratch of stubble against my lips.

Scared to say goodbye, we push all grief away
with weak forced smiles that say:
"I love you. I love you,"

again and again, "I love you."
One last kiss. One last embrace.
"I love you."

I trace the contours of your face,
smile, belly, thigh –
"I love you. . ."

Leaving Blackrock
I sit on the Dart like a lost child,
picking at the plaster that has stuck you to my heart:

Picking at the edges. Flinching at the pain.
Afraid to grasp it firmly and rip it off
with one short, sharp, shock.

I've Already Loved you Forever

"The present,"
John says, "is just a moment.
A now.

The past and future
but patterns perceived,
one now after another.
Yet every now is an eternity
unto itself. Infinite."

"And so you see,
though I've already loved you
an infinity of eternities,

I will always love you forever."

Rêves de Venise

Waking from a Venetian dream,
I can still hear the soft wet slap on the courtyard steps
while in the distance a tenor's song echoes on the Palazzos,
bouncing off narrow canyons of brick and marble and stone
carried by the turquoise flow to my open window.

I see bridges suspended on sighs, carried aloft
on angel wings; watched by Madonnas with sad eyes
forever imprisoned in decaying walls.
They whisper silent prayers; flickering, candlelit,
as shadows drift along the slow canals.

Waking from a Venetian dream,
I hear the hard cold splatter of the rain,
drumming to the West wind's whistle,
leading a chorus of birdsong in my garden
where no fig tree grows.

I turn and touch you as you sleep
and kiss the warm marble
of your chest. You smile,
still dreaming of the Grand Canal.

Catnip

You are catnip
to me. You are.
Just one whiff and I'm off –
kissinanahuggin,
lickinanasuckin –
all the hidden nooks
and crannies;
nuzzling all those places
only I ever get to smell; whose scent
makes me swoon and want to roll
around with you like kittens in a meadow.

You are catnip
to me. You are.
Just one kiss, like the first
kiss, like the last
kiss

and I'm off again –

like that first
night, like last
night, and the night before

and last Saturday afternoon
and still I want you again,
still I want you

more.

I burrow into your arms,
curl between shoulder and neck;
and purring, fall asleep
with a smile on my face
and your taste
on my lips.

La Niña Milagrosa

"It is time to find your sealskin,"
she murmured, her whiskers tickling my ear.
"I've lost it,"

I mumbled in my dreams.
"It was stolen,"
she whispered back.

And though I did not want to hear her,
I knew that she was right.
"My soulskin!" I gasped and tumbled

back into the arms of the thief,
letting his soft breath lull me to sleep -
just one more time.

John's Panama hat

We spill into
the tiny shop,
crowded
and dark.
Laughing,
kissing,
bumping
into hats
and each
other.

"Per lui," I say.
"A Panama."

She nods. "Cosi?"
Crisp brim.
Black band.
Too wide.
"Cosi?"
Too high.
"Cosi?"
Too flat.
"Cosi?"
Too small.

Finally,
she smiles.
Holds it out
like a crystal flute of Prosecco on a silver tray: "This one."

Lonely Heaven

"It's heaven in your bed," he says
softly kissing my neck,
"but only when you're in it."

I stretch. Pull away.
Sigh into pillows –
still heaven, but lonely.

He takes me back in his arms.
I melt into his chest. Cling
like moss to rock.

Angels call us back
beyond the stars. I whisper
as my eyes close:

"Please God, make it last."

Conundrum

I.

Because you came home late Tuesday night
Because you were drunk and annoying

Because you promised to put out the rubbish
Because you forgot it Wednesday morning

Because on Saturday you promised to mind me
Because you got drunk and annoying instead

Because you pretended that nothing had happened on Sunday morning
Because you pretended that nothing had happened on Monday evening

Because you claimed ignorance today
Because you'll claim innocence tomorrow

Because the road to domestic hell is paved with good intentions

II.

Because you make me write poems about love
Because with you bliss is only a bed away

Because every cell of your body is in tune with mine
Because they hum in harmony as we sleep

Because I wilt when we are apart
Because I shed my sorrows in your arms

Because I love you
Because you love me

Because with you or without you
Is like with or without me

Because when I die you'll whisper: "I told you so."

III

Because I'm scared
Because I'm scared
Because I'm scared
Because I'm scared
Because I'm scared
Because I'm scared

Safe Haven

My hand slithers over shoulder,
slides down flank
slips under arm

to wrap itself around your wrist,
thumb hooked on the crook
of your palm.

Anchored,
I pull in close
the boat of my curves to your body's shore.

Harboured,
belly to buttocks,
our legs caressing, circle, entwine,

then untangle,
to lie side by side;
tidy as coiled rope on a pier.

WRITER

39

The Strap Hangs Ready by the Door

Searching for the tell-tale signs
That innocence can never know
Suspicion haunts the guilty mind

Spying through Venetian blinds
For hands in pockets, hands below
Searching for the tell-tale signs

Idle hands the devil finds
Who can tell where they might go?
Suspicion haunts the guilty mind

Under the covers of bed, books and rhymes
Rooting out sins before they grow
Searching for the tell-tale signs

Spitting the fruit and eating the rind
Bitter thoughts in every swallow
Suspicion haunts the guilty mind

Justice with Love is doubly blind
Unsoiled and pure as fresh fallen snow
Yet searching for the tell-tale signs
Suspicion haunts the guilty mind

Advice to a Creative Writing Student
for Camy

Sit still
Wait
Listen to your heart beating
Feel the breeze
Smell the message it carries
Forget everyone else
Forget yourself

Write

You Won't Find this One in the Bible

When Jesus went into the river
he did not drift aimlessly like a leaf carried
powerless to the sea.

His unnatural buoyancy
allowed him to sit as if on a chair
driven by heavenly grace,

a beatific smile on his face,
waving at the beasts, birds and startled disciples
as he floated serenely by.

This miracle was never recorded
as it was thought to be rather a silly stunt
and much less dignified than walking on water.

Anam Cara
for Sue

And so it was that in the last hour,
of the last day, of my stay
in Anam Cara, I went down to the cascade.

I chose my path carefully, from seaview room to gallery,
from nest through the conservatory and into the dark woods,
holding tight the rope so as not to slip in the mire.

I sat on soft moss seat, legs stretched on grey rock
and thought: how conveniently placed
Nature is.

There, by rushing waters' fall, I found my heartsoul,
long lost in the clutter of so many years.
I dusted it off, washed it with tears

and listened to it sing.

Ten Steps to Stay Sane
for Ray

1.

Eat well
Better yet - cook well
Make bread by hand regularly
(and cakes, and jam)
Understand the importance of dessert

(Eat ice cream -
Not a lot
but seasonally
and from time to time
out of season)

2.

Listen to live music

(at least twice a month
Better yet - play music
at least once a week)

3.

Have a lot of fulfilling sex

4.

Remember to take advantage of summer afternoons
to sleep in the sun
and winter evenings
to doze by the fire

5.

Live somewhere beautiful

(If you can't live somewhere beautiful
find somethingplace beautiful
to look at every day)

6.

Love a lot

7.
Have a relationship with as many species of animals as you can manage

(If you can't have a dog or a cat or a horse or a pet rabbit –
buy a bird feeder)

Notice hawks
on the highway
and rats in the river

8.
Watch the plants
grow and die and grow
with the seasons

9.
Get to know lots of people
Have many acquaintances
Love your family and friends
Have one great love
Talk to them
On the bus
In the waiting room
On the phone
Or in bed

10.
Say I love you
and sleep
a lot.

Cork's Changed

Stuck in traffic in Douglas
on a cold dark February evening,
I watch a door fly open:
a young builder in jogging pants
saunters out of the offy with a 6 pack of Dutch Gold
and runs down the street to get drunk at home.

Earlier, the girls at the check-out
chatted to each other over my head
in foreign tongues normally not heard
this far west of the Danube. Laughing,
they flirted with the Polish guy behind me
and I felt shut out in my own Centra.

(When Marks and Sparks opened on Pana
I didn't like it. I didn't like
the aspirations of the oppressor invading Lee kitchens,
replacing pig trotters and spiced beef with guacamole and Thai green curry.
Now it's my favourite
because the Ladies at the check-out are all Irish and call me pet
as they scan my British prepacked food.)

Driving home late that night
I stop for petrol in Wilton.
It's open 24/7 and the black guy
locked behind the glass shop front
makes me laugh with his Afro-Corkonian wit.

Saltimbanques
for the Lucent

This is my tribe. These are my people.
Not by blood or geography,
but by the flamboyance,

finery and feathers that mark
us as those who dared to run
away with the circus;

to paint our faces,
to fly through the air,
to tumble and twirl,

to juggle your dreams;
to the beating of drums
in the flickering flames,

singing: *Life is serious,*
but Art is fun. Fuck Art.
Let's Dance!

Artists' Exemption
for Anto

We're artists,
God Damn it!
Not robots. Not sheep.

Not doctors. Not lawyers.
Not Statesmen.
Not priests.

We're artists,
God Damn it!
Not tailors, nor traders.

Not butchers. Not bakers.
Not soldiers, nor sailors.

Not builders, nor buyers.
Not gurus. Not Saints.
Not Bishops. Not bankers,

nor all of those wankers
who don't understand
they've just one life to live.

We're artists
God Damn it!
Just give us some space:

A room of our own
Our paper. Our paints.
Our pens and pianos.
Our Sunsets on Fire.

Just tip toe out quietly
And leave us alone.

We're artists,
God Damn it!

Where else will you get
Your songs and your paintings?
Your plays and your poems?
And movies? And comics?
And novels and stories?

We're artists,
God Damn it!
We work in the dark.
We give what we have.
Our doubt is our passion.
Our passion is our task
and the rest is the madness of Art. *

* "From Henry James, "The Middle Years" (1893)"

Wallflower

When I saw you up there, dancing on the table
my instinctive need was to join you –
Your spectacular dexterity thrilled me.
Your nimble feet enthralled me.
Your strong hands called me.
Your green eyes undressed me.
But as I stood up (my heart pounding)
a tall red head behind me
clamped a long stemmed rose in her teeth,
tossed her hair and leapt up beside you;
leaving me standing stranded,
longing and lost;
pretending to smile,
hiding my shame behind polite
prim applause.

Not a Cigarette

"This is not a cigarette,"
she says, passing round the joint
over beer cans and empty wine
bottles tossed by the party tide
like boats abandoned in the bay
beyond the coffee table shore.
Smoke words drift above our heads,
recumbent on cracked leatherette.
We sit and watch them form
and fade and float away on a bass wave
out the door.
"This is not a cigarette," he says,
handing me the joint over
flowing ashtrays, spilling beer and bottles
into puddles of wine on the canstrewn floor.
"This is not a cigarette," I say
and pull hard on the joint.
Lying back on leatherette,
I exhale slow to make my point.
The smoke words waft and wane away...
... I catch their drift and make them stay.
I hook'em.
Reel them in
and own 'em.

Say: "This is not a cigarette. It's a late-night partypoem."

For Sharon

It's in the light
between shadows
as the clouds race the valley

It's in the silence
between the crow's caw
and the wind's rush

It's in the stillness
between the last heartbeat
and the next breath

that the poet
finds the

poem.